I WANT

COMICS BY JASHORN

mc Marshall Cavendish
Editions

Published by Marshall Cavendish Editions
An imprint of Marshall Cavendish International

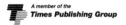

A member of the
Times Publishing Group

Other Marshall Cavendish Offices:
Marshall Cavendish Corporation, 800 Westchester Ave, Suite N-641, Rye Brook, NY 10573, USA • Marshall Cavendish International (Thailand) Co Ltd, 253 Asoke, 16th Floor, Sukhumvit 21 Road, Klongtoey Nua, Wattana, Bangkok 10110, Thailand • Marshall Cavendish (Malaysia) Sdn Bhd, Times Subang, Lot 46, Subang Hi-Tech Industrial Park, Batu Tiga, 40000 Shah Alam, Selangor Darul Ehsan, Malaysia

Marshall Cavendish is a registered trademark of Times Publishing Limited

National Library Board, Singapore Cataloguing in Publication Data

Name(s): Jashorn.
Title: I want comics / by Jashorn.
Description: Singapore : Marshall Cavendish Editions, [2023]
Identifier(s): ISBN 978-981-5066-92-0 (paperback)
Subject(s): LCSH: Caricatures and cartoons. | Singaporean wit and humor, Pictorial.
Classification: DDC 741.5695957--dc2

Printed in Singapore

To my most Heaven-sent younger sister & God.
Thank you both for being the reason why this book exists.

66 If you think humor died when Gary Larson (*The Far Side*) quit, and miss witty and irreverent comic jokes that can catch you by surprise at every turn, get this book! I witnessed how dedicated this humorist toiled to uncover jokes buried in word play and zany situations over years, and bring back laughter from the golden age of one-frame punchlines. 99

Otto Fong
Cartoonist, Illustrator

66 Who is Jashorn? He is a friend from my salad days, who became my Facebook friend, who one day started drawing Gary Larson-esque cartoons and posted them online and tagged me and did so so obsessively that we cried: "Get these out somewhere already!" And he did. Marvellous! 99

Gwee Li Sui
Poet, writer, critic

FOREWORD

I've been drawing since cartoons were a fixture on Saturday mornings. As a six-year old, my parents were surprised that I was copying Transformer robots from the TV with a pencil instead of watching with an open jaw at proceedings as most did. They tried bringing me to drawing competitions but these were a big failure as all this attention-fickle kid did was stare at Star Wars action figures at the next door toy store window.

It wasn't till high school that I found my stride in art class. Practice warnings from a stern teacher meant my right hand finally got the practice it needed from weekly classes. Again, my attention strayed again toward Marvel comics and a series of comics that grabbed my heart and made my cheeks constantly smirk. Both *Bizarro and The Far Side* comics had such a huge impact on my insides (heart, ribs and all) that I didn't realize a college degree in psychology and a short stint in marketing communications couldn't keep the child in me from trying my hand at doing the same thing Mr Larson did years after my adult career.

A simple dare from one of my church friends was all it took.

What started as fan art on Instagram soon evolved into work after work of my own as I came up with jokes like a gambling machine on steroids. Next thing I knew I was drawing single panel comics like a swimmer who went for daily Olympics training.

Thankfully, I loved it. After half a decade of enjoyable drawing, I was asked if a compilation of comics in a book was in order. I jumped at the opportunity.

Gladly I now present to you, my first half decade of comics. Have fun. :D

"Hi there!! May I be
your Professional Piggy Bank?"

"Think you got it confused, Son. They call me Mountain Bike Guru for my Bike Repair advice, not Life lessons in exchange for your Bike!"

What we Parents really.....REALLY feel like doing to them sometimes.

Dave and Sam's addiction to their game consoles regularly kept them safe in the Eye of the Storm.

Technique is vital when you're showing off to that Sexy Older Gal you like.

Petrol Prices can be the Scariest.

Eve expresses her
Newfound Hate of Snake.

Nothing beats a Fresh Sand-wich.

"Hey there, you the New Chick around here?"

It's not easy being a Knight in Shining Armour this modern day and age.

Fish numbers get vague when Jake the Snake takes the nearby cake.

"Oh dammit! Isn't it obvious??
They're all in there!!"

A simple trip to the Toy store instantly made Donald the most feared Duck in the Swamp.

For reasons unknown, Samantha's nightlife was always filled with weird European Guys who all wanted a Bite of her.

The Diver gave Tiger Sharky a hand with his first ever Selfie.

It wasn't easy convincing the rest that I was a Real Cowboy.

The Japanese Soccer team greatly improved in Defence
after their National Sumo Wrestling team was recruited.

Most Historians were unaware that
King Arthur was the first ever Eco-Terrorist
with his Magical Sword.

It was tough when Everywhere that Mary
went, the Lamb was sure to go.

It was always so Fun tying these fellas
together and running off.

"Your Honour, he was raised by Animals...
ANIMALS!! Can we expect him to see
eye to eye with the Law?"

Alice simply adored the New Egg she found.

Nobody knew that Excalibur was a Sword Handle, not a full Sword.

When Dr Banner runs out of Toilet Paper.

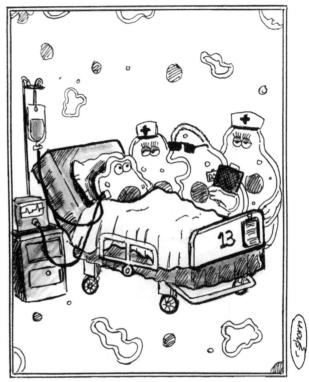

"I'm afraid we can't give you even a Single Cell transplant Sir. It would kill your Donor!"

Coral Carnivores in Chorus can be a Curse to the Community.

Much like upstairs, some Dogs are also Royalty downstairs.

Michelle was utterly Shocked when he placed his Hen on her Lap.

The Horror repeats itself every Single Day.

Stupid Vikings.

"Polly wants <u>your</u> Cracker."

Surgically approved Selfies.

Young Magnuto never understood why Needles in a Haystack were so difficult to find.

Nothing came between Daniel and his Anita who floated into his heart from the nearby Swamp.

Beachfront Properties at the North Pole got much less durable
and valuable with Global Warming.

My Boyfriend's mixed parentage always came in handy when
we wanted the Beach all to ourselves.

"Y'know, it's a nice change of pace. Everyone treats us like we're Bad Luck but these Guys always think they've struck the Lottery whenever they see us."

Eventually it proved impossible to avoid discussing the Elephant in the Room.

It was pretty obvious which Spiders in the area were Accountants in their previous lives.

A brilliant Bio-Engineer mocked by his peers, Prof Piggins had the last Laugh when his Pigs could fly.

What happens when you are Shipwrecked on an Island Archipelago of other Survivors.

Emily always wished she felt more like
a Black Sheep when visiting her In-Laws.

They never knew how Popular they were.

34

Teenage Stephanie never imagined waking up on the
Sexiest Hunkiest Giant Snail of her life.

Bob painfully regretted agreeing to the Free
Acupuncture session by the Mosquitoes.

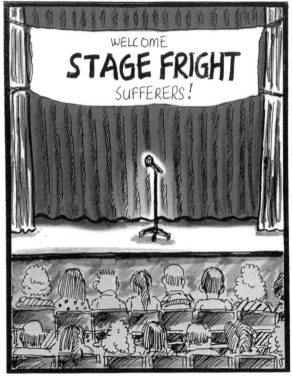

Getting Footwear is tough when
you have extra Big feet.

One thing great about late nite Vulture Beer
Parties are the Leftover Bottles you have
Fun with on subsequent mornings.

Being the Sheriff's dog meant Rex had inside information on local Crime.

Life begins at Reception.

The Bat of Gotham never imagined having such a small pesky Assistant in his life.

"Will. You. Stop. Eating. In. Bed."

The Smartest way to get rid of your Pesky Fleas for good is to give them a comfy New Home.

Richard hated his wife's Home-grown Vegetables.

".....TAKE US TO YOUR LEADER!!!"

Tranquility came upon our Nerves as we
started Surgery on Dan's Birthday Cake.

"Y'know, why stay at the Lousy Swamp
and hunt Flies when we can stay here!!"

"Honey I seriously think we're losing
more and more Privacy if we keep
meeting like this!"

"It's tough you know. Every Gal thinks
I'm a Predator because of these
Silly Fangs I have!"

In our line of work, some Nuts we deal with
are Sweet, some Salty. Most are Plain Nuts.

"Honey, i really don't like that Huge Bird outside – he keeps staring at us!!"

"Sir!! Sir!!! You left your Receipt behind!!"

Things got confusing for Immigration whenever the Invisible Man
and his family went on Vacation.

"I see......you will pay me for today's Session."

It's not easy ensuring that every Body's alright.

My Dad REALLY loved Dark Coffee.

It sometimes gets really frustrating when Parking is Full.

Most do not know that Vegetarian Vultures suffer from the most Mouth Ulcers in the World.

As a Floral Marriage Counselor,
my job was simple: keep Couples who
grew apart, together!

"Man, you sure? Those are three really,
REALLY little Pigs...!!!"

Spider Poetry Recitals are scary — they involve conquering both Stage Fight and Fear of Heights!

Given too many stolen Helmets, the Castle near the Farm soon closed its Armory.

Never play your Game Console so loudly at night that even the
Monsters below your Bed protest.

It is important to notice the right Signs on the Road to lasting Love.

"….Egyptian PRISON INMATE this one must be!!"

"Sorry Boss, I'm afraid you need new Staff again. I'm the only one left and I handle Trapdoor logistics."

"Yikes, when's the last time he actually washed his Behind?"

Less Kingdom Crime meant it was more Torture preparing Food Ingredients than Human Heads.

Uh-Oh.

Not everyone practices Road Courtesy.

Ghost Writer's Block

Some Microscopes can be really Paranoid with other On-lookers.

Love is Blind.

"Haha!! Told ya he's a Natural! Just wait till he kills the Rest of the Competition!"

"Awww Mom. Oh please!! Can't we just keep him? He followed me all the way Home!"

Being on the Hunt wasn't easy.

Things can get very Stressful for Mutant Scallops who escape from Home Labs.

The painful 6-week Race to the Summit was nowhere as painful as losing to a 5-minute Skydive.

Bob and Dave subsequently had the worst Sleep Hibernation of their Lives, ever.

"I'm deeply sorry Mr Claus. Your Reindeer's Nose Allergy is really an incurable ailment."

It was Raining like crazy but the darn Umbrella I got just ….wouldn't ….work!!!!

He just knew he had to get there first before the Rest.

Never buy Swedish Doghouses.

Where the Cow first jumped over the Moon.

They were the Best in Oil Sales.

"......Trick or Treat."

"Oh c'mon!! He's been at it for so looong.
The least we can do is help him!!"

"....come out, come out, wherever you are!!!"

Sometimes it really helps to be Multilingual.

We soon realized the New Flies we got from the Dump
were less than Digestible.

Flea Property Developers

Nobody imagined the Greedy Residents of a Frog Farm were actually behind the Global Bat Virus Pandemic.

"Yes we have the Intruder surrounded Sir. But he doesn't seem to know or care it's OUR Beach he's on."

A simple Dietary decision by the Mice doomed all Unicorns to extinction.

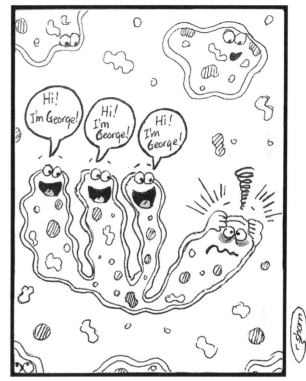

Catastrophic was the Self Discourse Self-Divided George had with himself.

"Oooh!! Don't ya just LOVE doing Morning Stretches here...!"

Where Smoked Duck comes from.

Complications ensued when Rapunzel's Prince was far more Overweight than she expected.

"HEY!!!! Watch where you're biting, you Moron!!"

Earth Day felt pointless when it was earth forever
for our Daily Food and Lives.

Fresh guys don't know Shit.

Sometimes it can be both.

Cloud usage can be Eternal.
So can the Fees.

Enough was enough. Rex was Sick and Tired of always being treated like a Dog by them.

"Geez....this is Sexual Harassment!!!"

Being Head Chef was enjoyable. Especially when the last Head Chef gave me a hand with my swift promotion.

Cat-Burglars

Legal Cross-Examination can be a really,
really stressful affair.

Contrary to popular belief, it was Two Wise Men, not three.

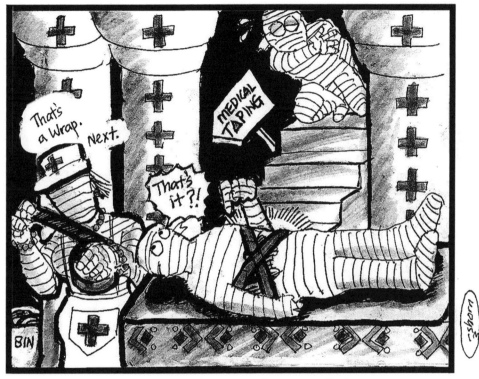

The Mummy Nurse was a Curse to all who
had encountered injuries worst.

Teaching each other the Birds and the Bees.

"Hey, what gives? Our Old Lady flew off as quickly as the Blue Guy flew in with that new Signboard."

"Hurry up. Your Lives are at Steak."

Hummingbird Practical Jokes.

Law-abiding citizen Robin Hoodlum
was sick and tired of all the Crime
committed in his name.

"Ah, the classic Fight or Flight response.
Next time stick to Flight. Not Fight IN Flight!"

We loved having our own
Private Parking Space.

It can be intense having Pizza
with Medical Precision.

"Don't get this the wrong way Honey.
Usually I may go for Leftovers,
but it's you I love."

"No no no. Be Patient! These things
usually come with a good Appetizer
too if you wait long enough!"

Sitting eye-to-eye from him, I soon realized he wasn't just the worst Boss anywhere but the most Evil being in the whole Universe.

Kill's parents never understood why he had few friends despite his killer sounding name.

Rex suddenly realized he shouldn't defecate
so much on to Mrs Truman's Flower Bed.

"Check this guy out, Marci ….
Black Ink Incontinence!!"

Hair does grow over time.

Being Headless also means you lack the Eyeballs and Neurology that come with it.

So they did.

We all need to survive.

"I can't help it, Stephen!! Can't help having this Crazy Urge to jump in and rip that large defenseless Cat to pieces…!!"

Dumb Antelopes.

The Jungle Hierarchy was altered
dramatically after Tarzan married Jane.

Emily was speechless when her Irritating
Amoeba of a Husband soon became
Two Irritating Husbands.

"Don't worry Mum. I'll be released by 5pm today when my Shift ends."

Life can be a Beach.

"I died for you!!! And every day you Idiot,
I'm STILL dying for you!!!"

"Try yer best to rest, OK? I'll be in every
few minutes to make sure you DON'T."

Big Foot's place in Legend began
with his swollen Left Sole.

"Well, one thing's for sure.
This is gonna take forever."

When Snakes slither like an Egyptian.

It gets mighty irritating when Mermaids love using your Boat for their daily exercises.

"Ha!! Best Repair ever –
it never breaks down ANYMORE!!!"

Mrs Shirley loved having a class full
of her own Teacher's Pets.

"Well, I guess I'll have the Root Beer Float!!"

"Your Turn."

It can be tough getting a single word outta some of these Fishy Witnesses.

"Man, it's Hot around here."

Cave-people in Hell.

Unfamiliar Terrain.

"How Scary High the Himalayas are?
Well just imagine me looking down at you
when you haven't done your Homework."

The Gun Control protesters faced Crowd
Control from Local Residents when things
got too Noisy for them.

"You moronic Brick! That's the fifth time this month!!! STOP THROWING YOURSELF AT ME!!"

"I really Suck, doc."

Piano lessons weren't easy with
Nagging Mothers and other Musicians
laughing across the room.

The Twins brought each other for Show and Tell and were Scarily good.

Upon seeing the Big Footwear before us, we swiftly decided to call off the Hunt.

"......please Wise One!!
I need... SOLUTION!!!"

"Hand it over."

Getting in can mean it's tough getting in every day.

It was tricky when Mum occasionally lost her Head during Sales at the Mall.

It was brief but boy, did we all enjoy having
a quick Refreshing Dip in the Mornings.

"Doris, I seriously think we should
consider Birth Control Pills,
not Condoms all the time."

Aladdin never knew his Magic Carpet was allergic to Human Perspiration.

My favorite Fishing Spot combined both my love of fishing and meeting nice Ladies.

"You know what's worse than being so Close? Being so Close and yet so Far Away."

What the Road of Marriage can feel like to so many of us.

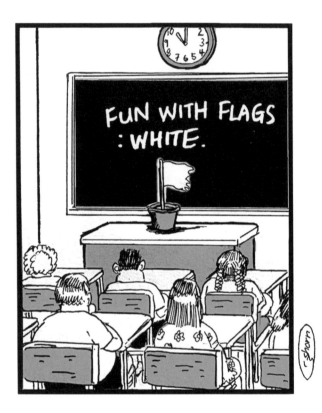

"I'm sorry, Sir. We think you MIGHT have some Broken Bones according to these X-Rays."

It can be scary to learn of the Birds and
the Bees from your own TV screens.

It's never easy waiting patiently
to be Dessert.

Joey realizes someone else has made him their Guard-dog without his consent.

Never trust any lowlife Property Agents who promise you and your spouse Privacy on a Petri-dish.

It gets embarrassing when Wolves in Sheep clothing have faulty clothes.

Why most Vampires usually avoid flying into Zoos.

Mrs Smith's desperate attempt to attract Teens from the next door Starbucks fell on Deaf Lips.

Do not use your Smartphones whilst eating. It has .....Consequences!

Space Exploration can be very daunting.

Why the Tower of Pisa leaned.

The indignities of Life as a
Robot Vacuum Cleaner.

About the Author/ Illustrator

Jashorn (aka Jason Lee) received his BA in Psychology from the National University of Singapore. Born in Singapore, Jashorn often haunted Yamaha Music Shops during his misspent youth as a French Horn player. Jashorn is notorious among his friends for making them constantly smile and for organizing his Lego Minifigures by Marvel films. When not writing, Jashorn enjoys exploring the Internet, and prefers to support his other hobbies of reading and drinking too much coffee

By the same author

WE WANT

COMICS BY JASHORN

Until the Virus, I never understood why my
dog was always begging me to go outside.